STAN GETZ OMNI

For B♭ Instruments • Transcribed Exactly from His Recorded Solos

ISBN 978-1-4803-9742-2

7777 W. BLUEMOUND RD. P.O. BOX 13819 MILWAUKEE, WI 53213

Visit Hal Leonard Online at
www.halleonard.com

STAN GETZ
(1927 – 1991)

Tenor saxophonist Stan Getz was nicknamed "The Sound" for his warm lyrical tone. He got his first big break playing in Woody Herman's band in the late 1940s. He had formed the Four Brothers saxophone group that was essential to the sound of Woody Herman's Second Herd. He soon became celebrated for his ballad playing.

Inspired by Lester Young, the Getz playing style was one of a relaxed approach, as opposed to the uptempo, bustling style of players such as Coleman Hawkins. Along the way, he fell into the common traps of alcohol and heroin, addictions that consumed most of his life. "The best way to play is completely sober, loose and happy...or unhappy" he once said.

Stan Getz was probably best known for his bossa nova work in the 1960s, especially with the hit single "Girl from Ipanema." The song helped to popularize the new musical style, which was originated by Brazilian musicians who combined traditional native folk music with a modern jazz bent.

Describing himself, Getz once said, "My life is music, and in some vague, mysterious and subconscious way, I have always been driven by a taut inner spring which has propelled me to almost compulsively reach for perfection in music, often – in fact, mostly – at the expense of everything else in my life."

You'll find these helpful features in this "omni" volume:

- 54 note-for-note transcriptions
- Meticulous easy-to-read notation
- Chord symbols to facilitate analyzing the solos and to provide a framework for accompaniment
- Rehearsal letters
- Transcription reference included with the songtitle
- Rhythmic styles and metronome marks

Airegin

from *"Artistry of Stan Getz Vol. 2"*
By Sonny Rollins

Sax Solo

All the Things You Are

from VERY WARM FOR MAY

from *"The Song is You"*

Lyrics by Oscar Hammerstein II
Music by Jerome Kern

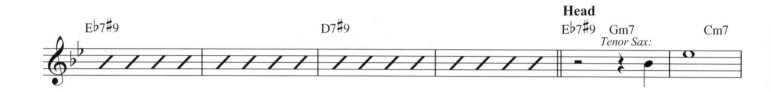

Autumn Leaves

from *"Jazz Café Presents Stan Getz"*

English lyric by Johnny Mercer
French lyric by Jacques Prevert
Music by Joseph Kosma

Bahia
(Na Baixa Do Sapateiro)
from *"The Essential Stan Getz"*
By Ary Barroso

Billie's Bounce
(Bill's Bounce)
from *Stan Getz and J.J. Johnson "At the Opera House"*
By Charlie Parker

Sax Solo ends

Trombone Solo

But Beautiful

from *"Stan Getz & Bill Evans"*
Words by Johnny Burke
Music by Jimmy Van Heusen

Blue Skies

from BETSY
from *"Blue Skies"*
Words and Music by Irving Berlin

(Rhythm section goes to double-time feel)

(Rhythm section resumes 4 feel)

Piano Solo

Sax Solo ends

Bass Solo

Head

Bass Solo ends

Blues in the Closet
from "At the Opera House"
By Oscar Pettiford

Trading with Trombone

Budo
from *"Complete Roost Recordings"*
By Miles Davis and Bud Powell

Sax Solo

Captain Marvel
from *"The Essence of Stan Getz"*
By Chick Corea

Come Rain or Come Shine

from ST. LOUIS WOMAN
from *"Pure Getz"*

Words by Johnny Mercer
Music by Harold Arlen

Sax Solo

69

Con Alma
from *"Yours and Mine"*
By John "Dizzy" Gillespie

Conception
from *"Quintessence"*
By George Shearing

Sax Solo

Detour Ahead
from *"Getz for Lovers"*
By Herb Ellis, John Frigo and Lou Carter

Confirmation

from *Stan Getz and Albert Dailey "Poetry"*

By Charlie Parker

Desafinado

from *"Stan Getz and Charlie Byrd Jazz Samba"*
Original Text by Newton Mendonça
Music by Antonio Carlos Jobim

Dizzy Atmosphere

from *"Quintessence: Vol. 1"*

By John "Dizzy" Gillespie

Outro

Drum Break

Drum Break ends

Doralice

from *"Getz/Gilberto"*

By Antonio Almeida and Dorival Caymmi

Early Autumn

from *"The Definitive Stan Getz"*
Music by Ralph Burns and Woody Herman

(Strings)

East of the Sun

(And West of the Moon)

from *"The Definitive Stan Getz"*

Words and Music by Brooks Bowman

Exactly Like You

from *"Diz and Getz"*

Words by Dorothy Fields
Music by Jimmy McHugh

Like Someone in Love

from *"The Steamer" World Record Club T341*

Words by Johnny Burke
Music by Jimmy Van Heusen

Head

Funkallero

from *"Stan Getz and Bill Evans"*
Music by Bill Evans

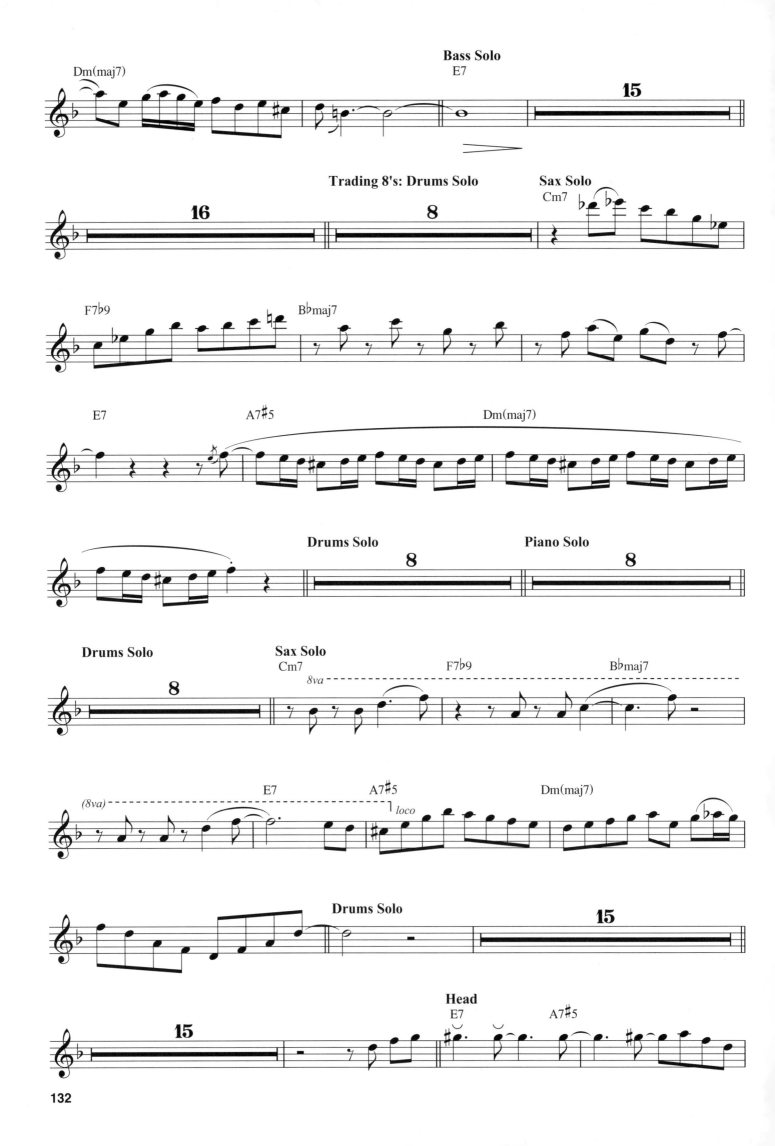

The Girl from Ipanema

(Garôta de Ipanema)

from *"Getz/Gilberto"*

Words and Music by Antonio Jobim and Vinicius de Moraes

I Remember You

from the Paramount Picture THE FLEET'S IN
from *"Serenity"*

Words by Johnny Mercer
Music by Victor Schertzinger

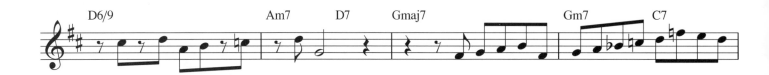

I Want to Be Happy

from *"Stan Getz and Oscar Peterson Trio"*

Words by Irving Caesar
Music by Vincent Youmans

Sax Solo

Move

from *"Complete Roost Recordings"*

By Denzil De Costa Best

My Ideal

from the Paramount Picture PLAYBOY OF PARIS
from "Quintessence Vol. 1"

Words by Leo Robin
Music by Richard A. Whiting and Newell Chase

Night and Day

from *"Stan Getz and Bill Evans"*
from GAY DIVORCE
Words and Music by Cole Porter

A Night in Tunisia

from "Poetry"

By John "Dizzy" Gillespie and Frank Paparelli

O Grande Amor

from *Stan Getz and Chet Baker "The Stockholm Concerts"*

Words and Music by Antonio Carlos Jobim and Vinicius de Moraes

Of Thee I Sing

from *"The Essential Stan Getz"*

Music and Lyrics by George Gershwin and Ira Gershwin

One Note Samba

(Samba De Uma Nota So)
from *"Stan Getz and Charlie Byrd Jazz Samba"*
Original Lyrics by Newton Mendonça
English Lyrics by Antonio Carlos Jobim
Music by Antonio Carlos Jobim

Quiet Nights of Quiet Stars

(Corcovado)
from "*Stan Getz w/Laurindo Almeida*"
English Words by Gene Lees
Original Words and Music by Antonio Carlos Jobim

Pennies from Heaven

from *"The Essential Stan Getz"*

Words by John Burke
Music by Arthur Johnston

Samba Dees Days

from "*Jazz Samba*"

By Charlie Byrd

Só Danço Samba

(Jazz 'n' Samba)

from *"Jazz Samba Encore!"*

Words by Vinicius de Moraes
Music by Antonio Carlos Jobim

Seven Steps to Heaven
from *"Final Concert Recordings"*
By Miles Davis and Victor Feldman

Sippin' at Bells
from *"Pure Getz"*
By Miles Davis

Softly, as in a Morning Sunrise

from THE NEW MOON
from *"People Time"*

Lyrics by Oscar Hammerstein II
Music by Sigmund Romberg

Head (2nd half)

Freely

Stella by Starlight

from *"Stan Getz Plays"*

from the Paramount Picture THE UNINVITED
Words by Ned Washington
Music by Victor Young

The Song Is You

from MUSIC IN THE AIR
from "The Song Is You"

Lyrics by Oscar Hammerstein II
Music by Jerome Kern

Stuffy
from "At Nalen"
By Coleman Hawkins

Summertime

from PORGY AND BESS®
from *"The Definitive Stan Getz"*
Music and Lyrics by George Gershwin,
DuBose and Dorothy Heyward and Ira Gershwin

Tune Up

from *"Poetry"*
By Miles Davis

Very Early

from "Pure Getz"
Music by Bill Evans

What Am I Here For?

from *"The Essence of Stan Getz"*

By Duke Ellington

Vivo Sonhando
(Dreamer)
from *"Getz/Gilberto"*
Words and Music by Antonio Carlos Jobim
English Lyrics by Gene Lees

The Way You Look Tonight

from "*Stan Getz Plays*"

from SWING TIME

Words by Dorothy Fields

Music by Jerome Kern

Where or When

from BABES IN ARMS
from *"Best of the Verve Years, Vol. 2"*

Words by Lorenz Hart
Music by Richard Rodgers

Wrap Your Troubles in Dreams

(And Dream Your Troubles Away)
from *"Quartets"*
Lyric by Ted Koehler and Billy Moll
Music by Harry Barris

Sax Solo

You Stepped Out of a Dream

from the M-G-M Picture ZIEGFELD GIRL
from *"Quartets"*
Words by Gus Kahn
Music by Nacio Herb Brown

Yardbird Suite ✓

from *Stan Getz and Chet Baker "Live at Haig 1953"*
By Charlie Parker

Trumpet Solo
Sax continues under trumpet:

280

Bass Solo

Trumpet & Sax Trade 4's with Drums

Yesterdays

from *"Voyage"*
from ROBERTA
Words by Otto Harbach
Music by Jerome Kern